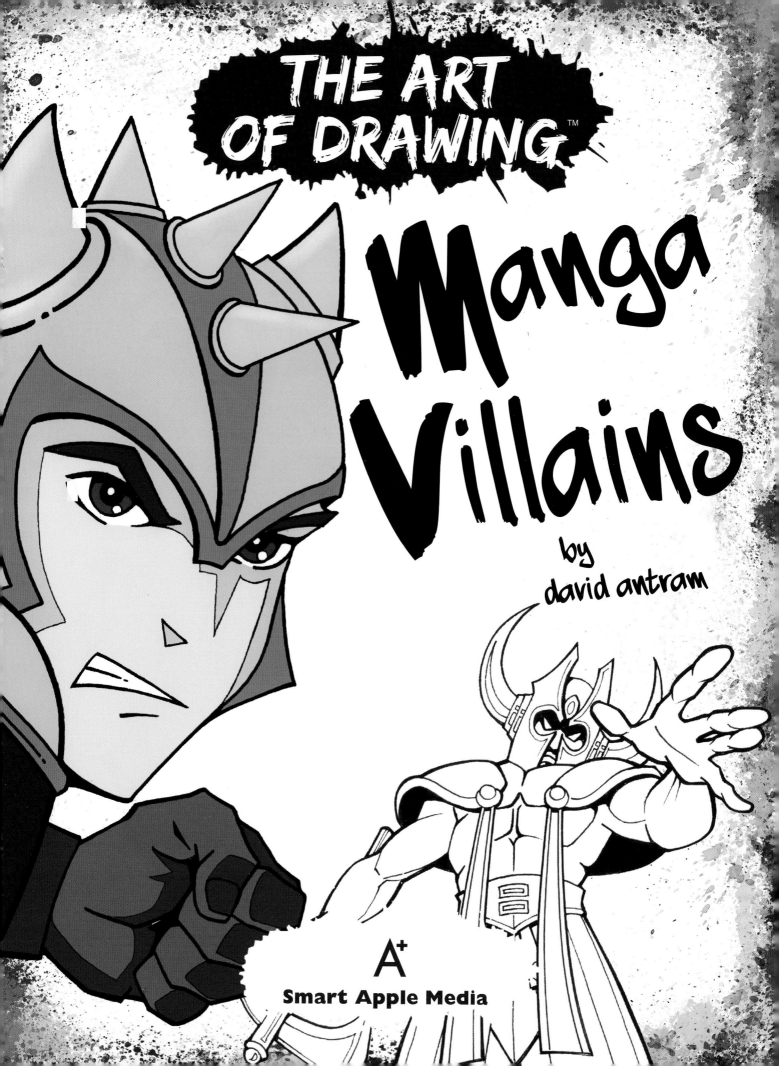

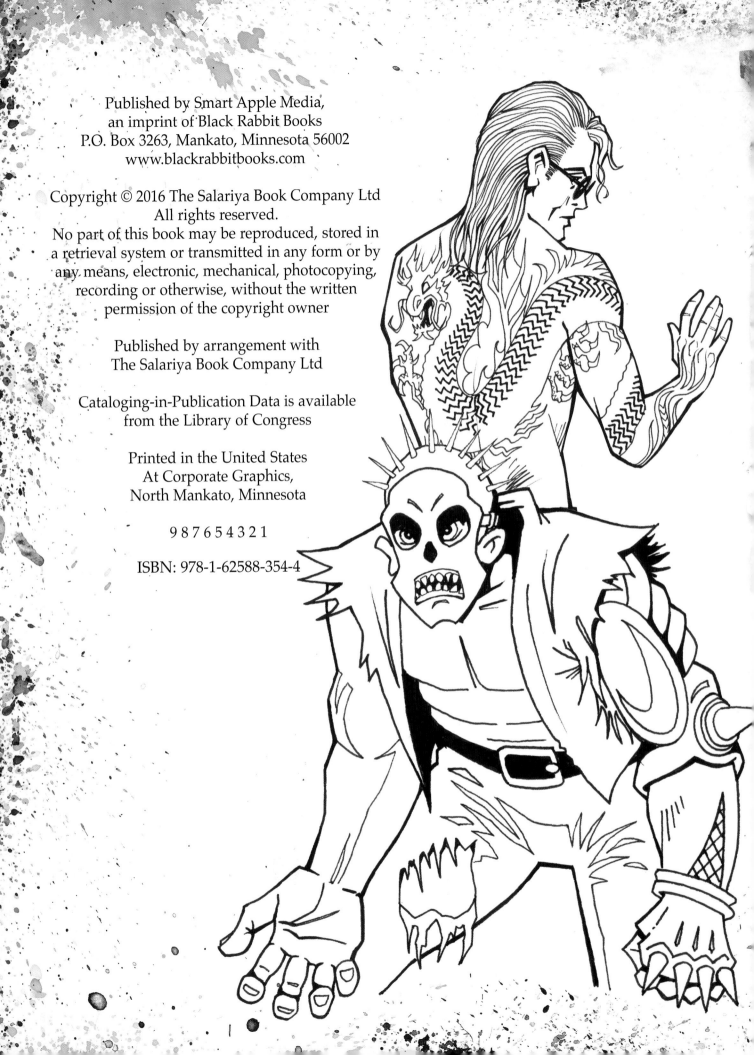

Published by Smart Apple Media,
an imprint of Black Rabbit Books
P.O. Box 3263, Mankato, Minnesota 56002
www.blackrabbitbooks.com

Published by arrangement with
The Salariya Book Company Ltd

Cataloging-in-Publication Data is available
from the Library of Congress

Printed in the United States
At Corporate Graphics,
North Mankato, Minnesota

9 8 7 6 5 4 3 2 1

ISBN: 978-1-62588-354-4

contents

making a start

The key to drawing well is learning to look carefully. Study your subject until you know it really well. Keep a sketchbook with you and draw whenever you get the chance. Even doodling is good—it helps to make your drawing more confident. You'll soon develop your own style of drawing, but this book will help you to find your way.

Try adding facial detail.

Practice drawing basic head and body shapes.

quick sketches

Try experimenting with different characters.

perspective

Perspective is a way of drawing objects so that they look as though they have three dimensions. Note how the part that is closest to you looks larger, and the part furthest away from you looks smaller. That's just how things look in real life.

The vanishing point (V.P.) is the place in a perspective drawing where parallel lines appear to meet. The position of the vanishing point depends on the viewer's eye level.

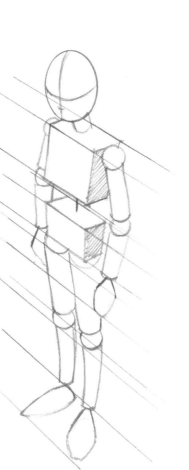

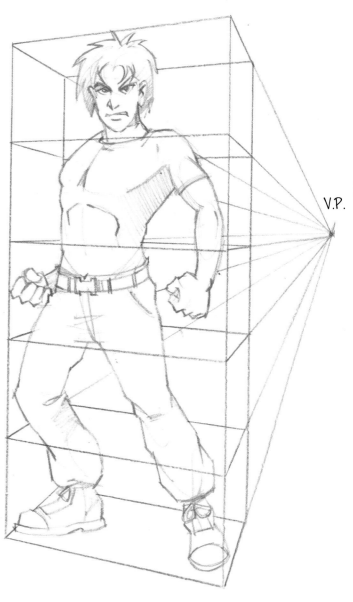

V.P.

two-point perspective drawing

Two-point perspective uses two vanishing points: one for lines running along the length of the subject, and one on the opposite side for lines running across the width of the subject.

In this drawing the vanishing points are low. This gives the impression that you are looking up at the figure—very dramatic!

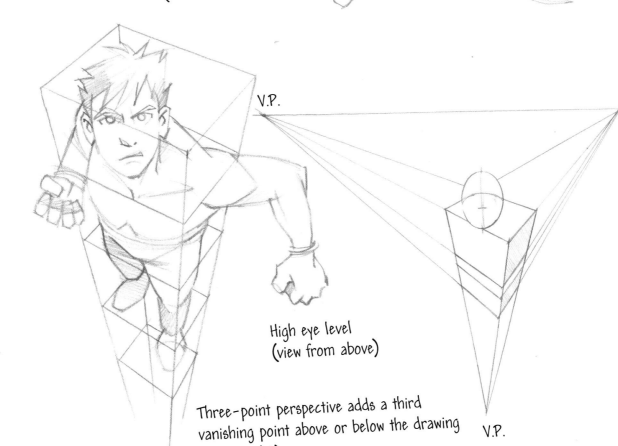

V.P.

Low eye level
(view from below)

V.P.

V.P.

V.P.

High eye level
(view from above)

Three-point perspective adds a third vanishing point above or below the drawing (above right.)

V.P.

V.P. = vanishing point

7

materials

Remember, the best equipment and materials will not necessarily make the best drawing—only practice will.

pencils

Try out different grades of pencils. Hard pencils make fine gray lines and soft pencils make softer, darker marks.

erasers

are useful for cleaning up drawings and removing construction lines.

paper

Bristol paper is good for crayons, pastels, and felt-tip pens. Watercolor paper is thicker; it is the best choice for water-based paints or inks.

Use this sandpaper block if you want to shape your pencil to a really sharp point.

inks

Use colored inks straight from the bottle or dilute them with water.

Ink

Mixing palette

felt-tip pens

Felt-tips usually come in sets of mixed colors. The ones that make very thin lines are called fineliners.

Fineliners

Dip-in pen nibs

Brushes

Correction fluid

Gouache

Watercolors

paints

Ordinary watercolors are translucent (see-through); gouache is not. Try other kinds of paints, too.

pens

Technical drawing pens have cartridges which can be refilled or replaced. Old-fashioned dip-in pens are much cheaper and come in many different styles and sizes.

Technical drawing pens

9

styles

Felt-tips come in a range of line widths. The wider pens are good for filling in large areas of flat tone.

Try different types of drawing papers and materials. Experiment with pens, from felt-tips to ballpoints, and make interesting marks. What happens if you draw with pen and ink on wet paper?

Ink silhouette

Silhouette is a style of drawing which mainly relies on solid dark shapes.

10

Pencil drawings can include a vast amount of detail and tone. Try different grades of pencil to get a range of light and shade effects in your drawings.

Lines drawn in **ink** cannot be erased, so unless you are very confident you may want to sketch your drawing in pencil first.

Hatching Cross-hatching

It can be tricky adding light and shade to a drawing with a pen. Use a solid layer of ink for the very darkest areas and cross-hatching (straight lines criss-crossing each other) for ordinary dark tones. Use hatching (straight lines running parallel to each other) for midtones.

11

body proportions

Heads in manga are drawn slightly bigger than in real life. Legs and hips make up more than half the overall height of the figure.

Drawing a stick figure is the simplest way to make decisions about a pose. It helps you see how different positions can change the center of balance.

Use points to identify joints such as knees and elbows, so when you add detail to your character these will be in proportion.

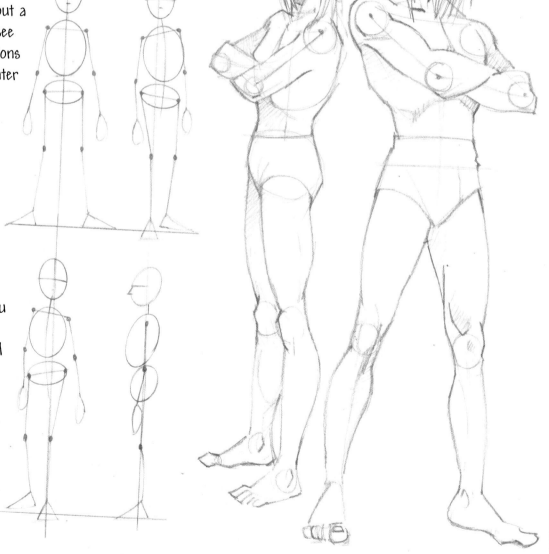

inking

Here's one way of inking over your final pencil drawing.

Refillable inking pens come in various tip sizes. The tip is what determines the width of the line that is drawn. Sizes include: 0.1, 0.5, 1.0, 2.0 mm.

Different tones of ink can be used to add depth to the drawing.
Mix ink with water to achieve the tones you need.

Correction fluid usually comes in small bottles or in pen format. This can be useful for cleaning up ink lines.

13

heads

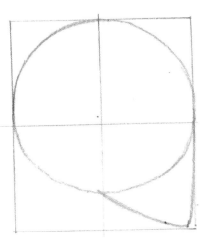

Manga heads have a distinctive style and shape. Drawing different facial expressions is very important—it shows instantly what your character is thinking or feeling.

1. Start by drawing a square with two center lines.

2. Draw the head, chin, and neck inside the square to keep the head in proportion.

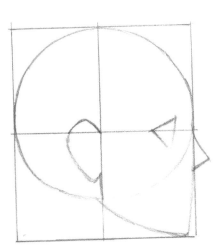

3. Use the markers created by the construction lines to draw the nose, eyes, and ear.

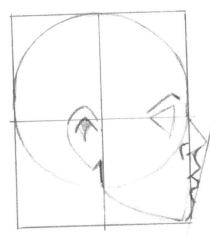

4. Add eyebrows and detail to the chin and mouth.

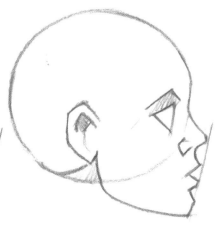

5. Add shade and remove your construction lines.

14

To create a head from the front, draw a rectangle and add the centerlines. Then add the oval shape of the head. Position the eyes, nose, and mouth using the centerlines as a guide. Finally add ears and extra facial details.

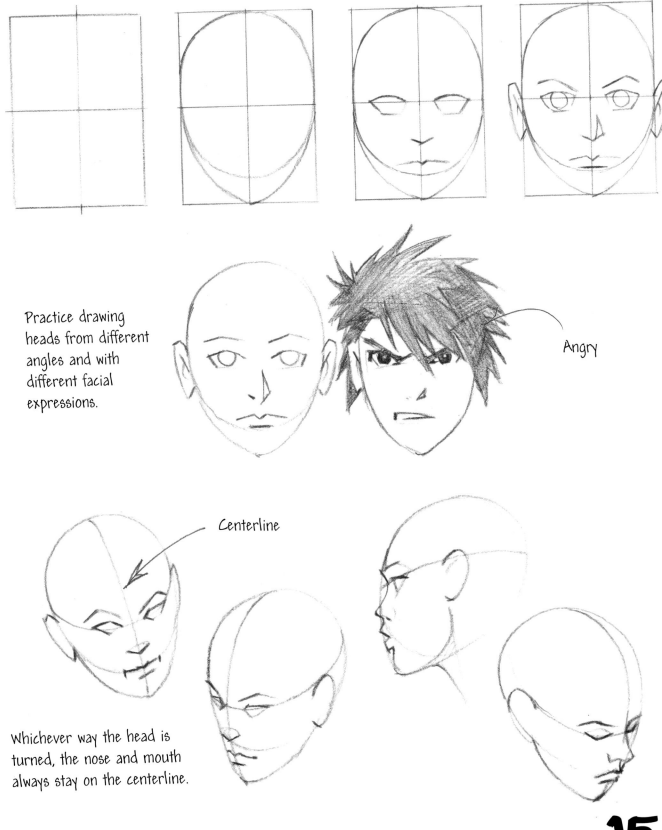

Practice drawing heads from different angles and with different facial expressions.

Angry

Centerline

Whichever way the head is turned, the nose and mouth always stay on the centerline.

light and shading

The light source for your subject will change how you add shade to your drawing. Stark contrasts in light and shade can create dramatic effects in your image.

The shaded areas of an object are determined by the direction of the light source.

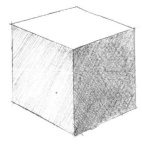

Here is a human head divided into sections to show how light from different sources effects the different areas of the head.

Light from above left

Light from above right

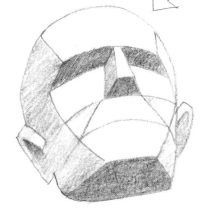

Light from below left

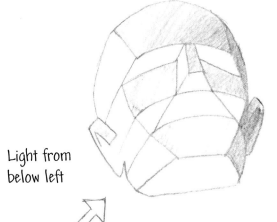

Light from below right

Draw a basic head shape using a box and construction lines (see page 15).

Now try out different light sources to see how it affects and changes your character's expression.

Adding light and shading to your drawings can transform your character's expression. Dark shadow around the eyes can give a dark, menacing look.

Light coming from below

Light coming from above

17

Wokou captain

Terrifying pirates, the Wokou are feared among sailors everywhere. When the Captain draws his sword his enemies cower in fear.

1. Draw ovals for the head, body, and hips. Add centerlines to divide the head vertically and horizontally.

Add a line for the sword.

2. Add lines for the spine and the angle of the hips and shoulders.

3. Draw stick arms and legs, with dots where the joints are. Add outline shapes for hands and feet.

Position the ears, nose, and mouth.

4. Using the construction lines as a guide, start to build up the main shapes and features.

Start to add shade to the darkest areas.

Draw little circles for the elbows and knees.

5. Draw the clothes, hair, and facial features. This is where your drawing really starts to come to life.

6. Use shading to add detail to the clothing and sword. Adding detail like creases in clothes can make your characters more realistic.

7. If you don't want your construction lines to show, erase them before you do the final shading and details.

8. Now finish all the little details such as the shading on the hair and clothes. Don't rush! The more carefully you do these finishing touches, the better your drawing will look.

Instead of shading your drawing you can try finishing your drawing in ink. Go over all outlines in ink and remove any pencil lines.

19

mighty warrior

This mighty warrior hides his face with a horned mask while defeating his enemies with his immense strength and power.

1. Draw a circle for the head, and ovals for the body, and hips.

2. Add lines for the spine and the angle of the hips and shoulders.

3. Draw stick arms and legs with dots for the joints.

Add lines for the fingers.

4. Use your guidelines to sketch in the facial features.

Draw little circles for the elbows and knees.

Add the ax.

Draw in the fingers. Remember that due to perspective they appear very large as they are closer to us.

5. Using the construction lines as a guide, start drawing in the main shapes of the body.

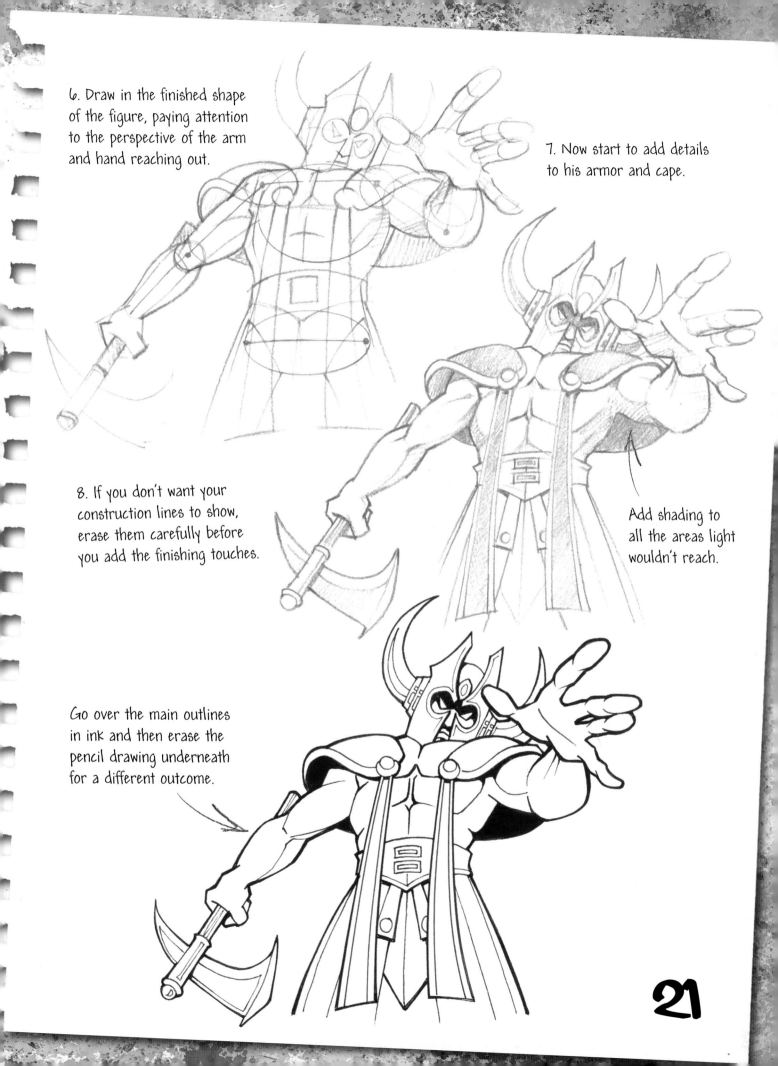

6. Draw in the finished shape of the figure, paying attention to the perspective of the arm and hand reaching out.

7. Now start to add details to his armor and cape.

8. If you don't want your construction lines to show, erase them carefully before you add the finishing touches.

Add shading to all the areas light wouldn't reach.

Go over the main outlines in ink and then erase the pencil drawing underneath for a different outcome.

21

sorcerer

The sorcerer's powerful spells strike fear in many. He dreams of one day ruling the world.

1. Draw ovals for the head, body, and hips. Add centerlines to divide the head horizontally.

2. Add lines for the spine and the angle of the hips and shoulders.

3. Draw stick arms and legs with dots where the joints are. Add outline shapes for hands and feet.

Add a line for the staff.

Sketch in the position of the sorcerer's book of spells.

Add the basic facial features.

Draw circles for the position of the shoulders, elbows, and knees.

4. Using your construction lines as a guide, add the main shapes and features of the figure.

22

5. Draw the clothes, hair, and facial features.

Adding detail like fringes on his jacket and an intricate belt buckle help bring the character to life.

6. Sketch in the sorcerer's many accessories.

7. Erase your construction lines if you don't want them to show.

8. Take plenty of time to finish the details of the face and body, adding shading to areas where light wouldn't reach.

You could try finishing your drawing in ink.

23

yakuza

The Yakuza are organized crime groups in Japan. This member has special tattoos which identify him as a top Yakuza member.

1. Draw different-sized ovals for the head, body, and hips.

2. Add a line for the spine and others to show the angle of the hips and shoulders.

3. Draw stick arms with dots for the joints and outline shapes for the hand.

Add a line to position the eyes and ears.

Sketch in the facial features.

4. Using your construction lines as a guide, draw the main shapes of the body.

Add the fingers.

Circle shows position of elbow.

5. Draw in more detail to the face and hair. Add more form to the body and begin to sketch out the tattoo.

6. Erase the construction lines if you want to, finish off all the remaining details.

Sunglasses give a mysterious look.

Don't forget to add details like his belt.

You can try finishing your drawing in ink.

25

princess aku

Aku is Japanese for "evil," and this princess certainly lives up to her name.

1. Draw different-sized ovals for the hips, body, and head.

2. Draw stick arms and legs in a sitting position, with dots for the joints. Sketch in simple shapes for the feet.

3. Draw in the main shape of the body, using the ovals to guide you.

Begin to sketch the outline of the opulent throne.

Drape robes over the throne.

4. Add details to the head, defining the shape of the facial features and hair. Begin to add detail to the robes and throne.

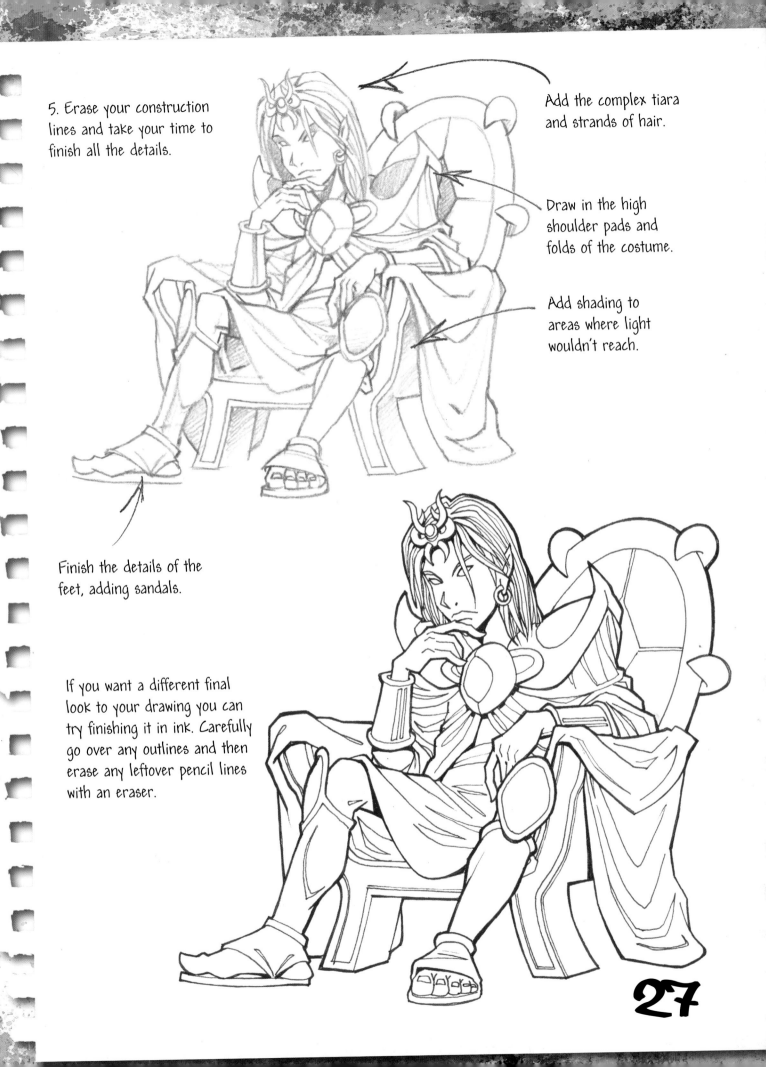

5. Erase your construction lines and take your time to finish all the details.

Add the complex tiara and strands of hair.

Draw in the high shoulder pads and folds of the costume.

Add shading to areas where light wouldn't reach.

Finish the details of the feet, adding sandals.

If you want a different final look to your drawing you can try finishing it in ink. Carefully go over any outlines and then erase any leftover pencil lines with an eraser.

mad scientist

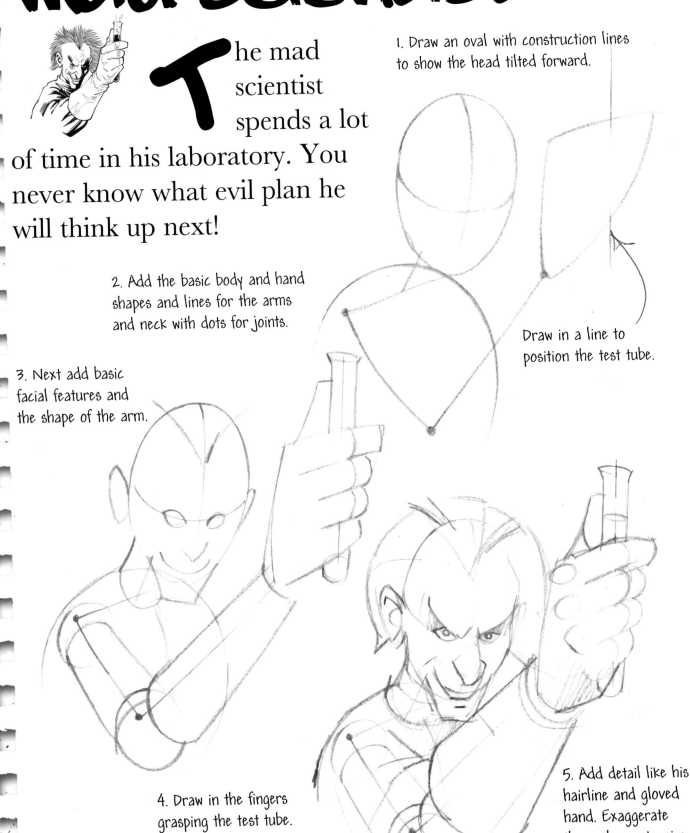

The mad scientist spends a lot of time in his laboratory. You never know what evil plan he will think up next!

1. Draw an oval with construction lines to show the head tilted forward.

Draw in a line to position the test tube.

2. Add the basic body and hand shapes and lines for the arms and neck with dots for joints.

3. Next add basic facial features and the shape of the arm.

4. Draw in the fingers grasping the test tube.

5. Add detail like his hairline and gloved hand. Exaggerate the eyebrows to give an evil look.

28

6. Finish the head by adding details such as messy hair and eyebrows.

7. Erase construction lines before adding final details such as shading and the highlights in the eyes.

Add liquid inside the test tube.

Add shaded areas to show the creases in the rubber glove.

Leave areas blank or erase back to white for highlights.

Here's the same drawing finished in ink. Decide which lines you want to ink in before you make any marks.

tero

Tero possesses super-human strength. He often struggles to keep his temper under control.

1. Draw the basic ovals and construction lines. Add dots where the joints will be.

2. Use your construction lines to add details to the limbs. Add the basic shape of the mask.

Sketch in the hair.

3. Using the construction line framework define the body shape. Add a jacket and fingers to the hands.

30

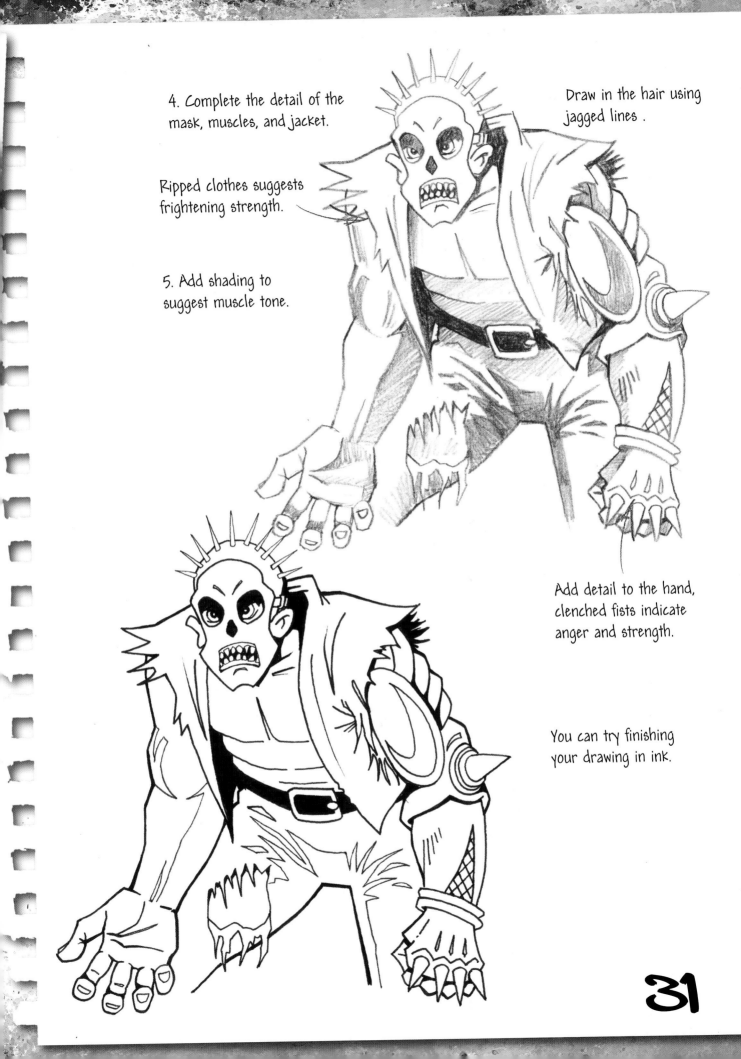

4. Complete the detail of the mask, muscles, and jacket.

Ripped clothes suggests frightening strength.

5. Add shading to suggest muscle tone.

Draw in the hair using jagged lines .

Add detail to the hand, clenched fists indicate anger and strength.

You can try finishing your drawing in ink.

31

glossary

Composition The positioning of the various parts of a picture on the drawing paper.

Construction lines Guidelines used in the early stages of a drawing which are usually erased later.

Cross-hatching A series of criss-crossing lines used to add shade to a drawing.

Hatching A series of parallel lines used to add shade to a drawing.

Manga A Japanese word for "comic" or "cartoon"; also the style of drawing that is used in Japanese comics.

Silhouette A drawing that shows only a dark shape, like a shadow, sometimes with a few details left white.

Three-dimensional Having an effect of depth, so as to look like a real character rather than a flat picture.

Tone The contrast between light and shade that helps to add depth to a picture.

Vanishing point The place in a perspective drawing where parallel lines appear to meet.

index